Burn Injuries
in Child Abuse

Portable Guides to
Investigating Child Abuse

Foreword

Our most defenseless children are the most likely to be burned intentionally. Child abuse burn victims are almost always under the age of 10 with the majority under the age of 2. Immediate identification of intentional burn victims by those individuals first responding to the call for assistance is crucial because most of the victims are unable to speak for themselves. It is also important that responsible caretakers not be unjustly accused.

In this guide you will find information that will assist you to distinguish intentional burns from accidental contact with hot objects. *Burn Injuries in Child Abuse* provides both guidance on determining the veracity of a caretaker's report by re-creating the incident and a burn evidence worksheet for use at the scene of an investigation. Information regarding the distinctions between immersion and contact burns is also included.

It is our hope that information in this guide will be of use to law enforcement as we all work to protect our children.

Original Printing May 1997

Second Printing June 2001

NCJ 162424

Although general awareness of the magnitude of child abuse is increasing, deliberate injury by burning is often unrecognized. Burn injuries make up about 10 percent of all child abuse cases, and about 10 percent of hospital admissions of children to burn units are the result of child abuse. In comparison with accidentally burned children, abused children are significantly younger and have longer hospital stays and higher mortality rates. The child burn victim is almost always under the age of 10, with the majority under the age of 2.

Children are burned for different reasons. Immersion burns may occur during toilet training, with the perpetrator immersing the child in scalding water for cleaning or punishment. Hands may be immersed in pots of water for playing near the stove. A person may place a child in an oven for punishment or with homicidal intentions.

Inflicted burns often leave characteristic patterns of injury that, fortunately, cannot be concealed. Along with the history of the burn incident, these patterns are primary indicators of inflicted burns versus accidental ones. Findings in response to the following questions can raise or lower the index of suspicion, helping to determine whether a burn was deliberately inflicted:

* Is the explanation of what happened consistent with the injury? Are there contradictory or varying accounts of the method or time of the "accident" or other discrepancies in the witnesses' descriptions of what happened?

* Does the injury have a clean line of demarcation, parts within or immediately around the injured area that are not burned, a burn pattern inconsistent with the injury account, or any other of the typical characteristics of an inflicted burn? Are the burns located on the buttocks, the area between the child's legs, or on the ankles, wrists, palms, or soles?

* Are other injuries present such as fractures, healed burns, or bruises?

* Are the child's age and level of development compatible with the caretaker's and witnesses' accounts of the injury?

* Was there a delay in seeking medical attention? Smaller burns may have been treated at home.

* Does the caretaker insist there were no witnesses, including the caretaker, to the injury incident?

* Do those who were present seem to be angry or resentful toward the child or each other?

A detailed history, including previous trauma, presence of recent illnesses, immunization status, and the status of routine medical care, is critical, as is careful documentation of the scene of the injury, including photographs and drawings. To investigate a burn injury:

* Stay focused on the facts in front of you and proceed slowly and methodically.

* Ask questions, be objective, and reenact the incident.

* Treat each case individually.

The incidence of further injury and death is so high in deliberate burn cases that it is critical for all concerned persons to be aware of the indicators of this form of child abuse.

The following descriptions provide information about the various types of accidental and nonaccidental burns children may incur.

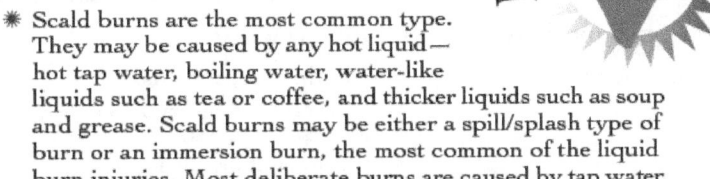

* Scald burns are the most common type. They may be caused by any hot liquid—hot tap water, boiling water, water-like liquids such as tea or coffee, and thicker liquids such as soup and grease. Scald burns may be either a spill/splash type of burn or an immersion burn, the most common of the liquid burn injuries. Most deliberate burns are caused by tap water.

* Contact burns are usually of the branding type and will mirror the object used to cause the injury—curling iron, steam iron, cigarette lighter, fireplace or hibachi grill, and heated kitchen tool or other implement.

Young children have thinner skin than adults; therefore, a child's skin will be destroyed more rapidly and by less heat. Thicker skinned areas of the body include the palms, soles, back, scalp, and the back of the neck. Thinner skinned areas are the front of the trunk, inner thighs, bottom of forearms, and the inner arm area.

It is important to work with the emergency medical personnel, who were probably the first persons to see the child's injuries, hospital personnel, and social services investigators.

Classification of Burns

The preferred classification of burns used by most physicians is "partial" or "full thickness" (see table 1, page 4). Only an experienced medical practitioner can make a determination of how deep a burn is, but there are some features of partial and full thickness burns that can be observed immediately after the incident.

* Patches of reddened skin that blanch with fingertip pressure and refill are shallow partial thickness burns. Blisters usually indicate deeper partial thickness burning, especially if the blisters increase in size just after the burn occurs.

* A leathery or dry surface with a color of white, tan, brown, red, or black represents a full thickness burn. The child feels no pain because the nerve endings have been destroyed. Small blisters may be present but will not increase in size.

Table 1

Classification of Burns

Classification	Characteristics
First degree	Partial thickness burns.
	* Characterized by erythema (localized redness).
	* Appear sunburn-like.
	* Are not included when calculating burn size.
	* Usually heal by themselves.
Second degree	Partial thickness burns.
	* Part of skin has been damaged or destroyed.
	* Have blisters containing clear fluid.
	* Pink underlying tissue.
	* Often heal by themselves.
Third degree	Full thickness burns.
	* Full skin has been destroyed.
	* Deep red tissue underlying blister.
	* Presence of bloody blister fluid.
	* Muscle and bone may be destroyed.
	* Require professional treatment.
Fourth degree	Full thickness burns.
	* Penetrate deep tissue to fat, muscle, bone.
	* Require immediate professional treatment.

Spill/Splash Injuries

These injuries occur when a hot liquid falls from a height onto the victim. The burn pattern is characterized by irregular margins and nonuniform depth. A key indicator to look for is where the scalding liquid first came into contact with the victim. Water travels downward and cools as it moves away from the initial contact point. When a pan of water is spilled or thrown on a person's chest, the initial contact point shows a splash pattern. The area below this point tapers down, creating what is called an "arrow down" pattern. This pattern is more commonly seen in assaults on adults than in assaults on children.

If the child was wearing clothing at the time of the injury, the pattern may be altered. This is why it is important to determine whether clothing was worn and, if possible, to retain the actual clothing. Depending on the material, the water may have been against the skin longer, which would result in a deeper injury and pattern. A fleece sleeper, for instance, will change the course of the water and hold the temperature longer in one area as opposed to a thin, cotton T-shirt.

Questions to ask in a scalding injury investigation include the following:

* Where were the caretakers at the time of the accident?

* How many persons were home at the time?

* How tall is the child? How far can he or she reach?

* Can the child walk and are the child's coordination and development consistent with his or her age?

* How much water was in the pan and how much does it weigh?

* What is the height to the handle of the pan when it is sitting on the stove (or counter, or table)?

* Was the oven on at the time (thus unlikely that the child could have climbed onto the stove)?

* Does the child habitually play in the kitchen? near the stove? climb on the cabinets or table?

* Has the child been scolded for playing in the kitchen? for touching the stove?

It is unusual for a child to incur a scald burn on his or her back accidentally, but it has happened. As in all burn investigations, factors other than location of the burn must be considered before concluding the injury was nonaccidental. Deliberate burning by throwing a hot liquid on a child is usually done either as punishment for playing near a hot object or in anger. However, the child may have been caught in the crossfire between two fighting adults and then been accused of having spilled the liquid accidentally.

Immersion Burns

Immersion burns result from the child falling or being placed into a tub or other container of hot liquid. In a deliberate immersion burn, the depth of the burn is uniform. The wound borders are very distinct, sharply defined "waterlines" with little tapering of depth at the edges. There is little evidence that the child thrashed about during the immersion, indicating that the child was held in place, and occasionally there may be bruising of the soft tissue to indicate that this is what happened.

Only children with deliberate immersion burns sustain deep burns of the buttocks and/or the area between the anus and the genitals. Many of these injuries involve toilet training or the soiling of clothing. There may be dirty diapers or clothing in the bathroom. The water in the bathtub may be deeper than what is normal for bathing an infant or child and may be so hot that the first responding adult at the scene is unable to immerse his or her own hand in it.

Several key variables must be observed in investigating immersion burns:

* **The temperature of the water.** Variables that must be taken into account include the temperature of the water heater, the ease with which it can be reset, and recent prior usage of water.

* **The time of exposure,** an unknown that can sometimes be estimated from the burn pattern and its depth.

* **The depth of the burn.** Several days may need to pass before the true depth of the burn can be determined.

* **The occurrence of "sparing"** (areas within or immediately around the burn site that were spared).

An adult will experience a significant injury of the skin after 1 minute of exposure to water at 127 degrees, 30 seconds of exposure at 130 degrees, and 2 seconds of exposure at 150 degrees. A child, however, will suffer a significant burn in less time than an adult.

When a child's hand is forced into hot water, the child will make a fist, thus "sparing" the palm and discounting the statement that the child reached into the pan of hot water for something. A child whose body is immersed in hot water will attempt to fold up, and there will be sparing in creases in the abdomen. Curling up the toes when the foot is forced into a hot liquid will spare part of the soles of the feet or the area between the toes. The area where the child was held by the perpetrator will also be spared. These flexing actions prevent burning within the body's creases, causing a striped configuration of burned and unburned zones, or a "zebra" pattern.

Deliberate immersion burns can often be recognized by one of the following characteristic patterns:

* **Doughnut pattern in the buttocks.** When a child falls or steps into a hot liquid, the immediate reaction is to thrash about, try to get out, and jump up and down. When a child is held in scalding hot bathwater, the buttocks are pressed against the bottom of the tub so forcibly that the water will not come into contact with the center of the buttocks, sparing this part of the buttocks and causing the burn injury to have a doughnut pattern.

* **Sparing of the soles of the feet.** Another instance of sparing occurs in a child whose buttocks and feet are burned but whose soles have been spared. If a caretaker's account is that the child was left in the bathroom and told not to get into the tub, and that the caretaker then heard screaming and returned to find the child jumping up and down in the water, the absence of burns on the soles of the child's feet is evidence that the account is not true. A child cannot jump up and down in hot water and not burn the bottoms of the feet.

* **Stocking or glove pattern burns.** Stocking and glove patterns are seen when feet or hands are held in the water. The line of demarcation is possible evidence that the injury was not accidental.

* **Waterlines.** A sharp line on the lower back would indicate the child was held still in the water. A child falling into the water would show splash and irregular line patterns. The waterline on the child's torso indicates how deep the water was.

An Evidence Worksheet for Immersion Burns and instructions for filling it out can be found at the end of this guide. This worksheet was developed to record data to help the doctor determine accidental or intentional injury. The information recorded on the worksheet is also helpful to the prosecutor in preparing the case and defeating potential defenses that may arise later in the investigation and trial. Developed with the assistance of a department of social services and several law enforcement child abuse investigative teams, the worksheet is a guideline and can be modified to suit particular investigative needs.

Contact Burns

Contact burns may be caused by flames or hot solid objects. Flame burns are a much less common cause of deliberate injury. When they do occur, they are characterized by extreme depth and are relatively well defined when compared with accidental flame burns.

When a child accidentally touches a hot object or the object falls on the child, there is usually a lack of pattern in the burn injury, since the child quickly moves away from the object. However, even brief accidental contact can cause a second-degree burn with the pattern of the object, for example, falling against a hot radiator or grate.

Distinguishing Nonaccidental from Accidental Contact Burns

Nonaccidental burns caused by a hot solid object are the most difficult to distinguish from accidental injuries. Cigarette and iron burns are the most frequent types of these injuries. Cigarette burns on a child's back or buttocks are unlikely to have been caused by walking into a lighted cigarette, and therefore are more suspect than burns about the face and eyes, which can occur accidentally if the child walks or runs into the adult's lighted cigarette held at waist height. Accidental burns are usually more shallow, irregular, and less well defined than deliberate burns. Multiple cigarette burns are distinctively characteristic of child abuse.

Purposely inflicted "branding" injuries usually mirror the objects that caused the burn (such as cigarette lighters and curling irons), and are much deeper than the superficial and random burns caused by accidentally touching these objects. Most accidental injuries with hot steam or curling irons occur when the hot item is grasped or falls. These are usually second-degree injuries and randomly placed, as might happen when a hot iron strikes the skin in multiple places as it falls. It is important to know where the iron was—for example, on an ironing board or on a coffee table at the child's height?

Another source of accidental burns is contact with items that have been exposed for prolonged periods to hot sun. Pavement in hot sun, which can reach a temperature of 176 degrees, can burn a child's bare feet; however, these are not likely to be deep burns. A child placed in a carseat that has been in a car in the sun can receive second- and even third-degree burns. Full thickness burns have also resulted from contact with a hot seatbelt buckle.

Key questions in this area are:

* Where is the burn injury and could the child reach the area unassisted?

* Does the child normally have access to the item (such as a cigarette lighter) that caused the injury?

* How heavy is the item and how strong is the child? For instance, is the steam iron a small travel-size one that a small child could lift or a full-size home model that might be too heavy?

* Is there any sparing that would be significant to the injury?

* How was the item heated and how long did it take to heat it to cause the injury?

* Is the injury clean and crisp, with a distinctive pattern of the object, or is it shallow or irregular, as from a glancing blow? Several cleanly defined injuries, especially on an older child, could indicate that the child was held motionless by a second perpetrator while the first perpetrator carefully branded the child.

* Are there multiple burns or other healed burns?

* Has the child been punished before for playing with or being too close to the hot object?

Skin Conditions That May Simulate Abuse

Investigators should be aware that it is sometimes difficult to distinguish between burns caused by abuse and certain diseases or medical conditions:

* **Cutaneous (skin) infections.** Some infections have patterns that may mimic deliberate injuries. Impetigo, severe diaper rash, and early scalded skin syndrome sometimes resemble a scald injury. A careful history, microbiological tests, and observation of the lesions over a 2- to 3-week period usually determine whether or not these are deliberate burn injuries or just infections.

* **Hypersensitivity reactions.** A substance in citrus fruits such as limes, when in contact with the skin and exposed to sunlight, can produce a form of photodermatitis with a pattern that resembles a splash burn. An allergic reaction causing a severe local skin irritation may be mistaken for a burn. Skin preparations such as

9

topical antiseptics can cause a similar burn appearance. Again, the exposure history will allow differentiation of these reactions from burns.

✳ **Marks left by folk remedies.** Moxibustion is an Asian folk remedy that entails placement of a hot substance, often burning yarn, on the skin of the abdomen or back, causing circular lesions that can be mistaken for other types of burn injuries. The practice of cupping, which is the placement in a cup or glass of a small amount of flammable substance that is ignited and placed on the skin, may cause a burn lesion. **Note:** Even when the cause of a burn injury is determined to be a folk remedy, investigators should exercise caution and carefully evaluate all circumstances surrounding the incident to determine whether the injury should be further investigated.

Helpful Investigative Techniques

The following investigative steps and techniques will help you and other professionals determine if burns have been purposely inflicted.

Medical Examination

The physical examination of all burned children includes careful evaluation of the entire skin surface for the presence of other signs of abuse such as:

✳ Healed burns.

✳ Multiple simultaneous burns.

✳ Bruises, slaps, and bite or whip marks.

✳ Evidence of sexual abuse.

Evaluation and documentation of the burn pattern should be precise. Multiple burns of varying ages and types that obviously could not have occurred from the same accident (for example, cigarette and scald burns or different types of scald burns) are strong indicators of child abuse. However, the absence of other injuries does not rule out child abuse, since 80 percent of deliberately inflicted burns are not associated with other trauma.

Long bone, chest, and a skull radiographic (x-ray) series (commonly called a "babygram") need to be performed on all burned children with suspected abuse. Unfortunately, there are no specific laboratory studies that will help distinguish deliberate from accidental burn injury.

Investigator's Checklist for Use in Suspected Cases of Deliberate Burn Injuries of Children

❏ Have you contacted the emergency response team?

❏ Have you contacted the child protective services team?

❏ Have you reviewed the medical findings with the appropriate medical staff?

❏ Have you carefully considered the suspicion index findings?

❏ Where was the primary care provider at the time of the incident?

❏ Where is the burn injury located on the child's body?

❏ How serious is the burn?

❏ Is the burn a wet contact burn or a dry contact burn?

❏ If the burn appears to have been caused by a dry source of heat, what is the shape of the burn and what object does it resemble?

❏ Have you completed the Evidence Worksheet for Immersion Burns?

❏ If the burn was produced by a hot liquid, was the child dipped or fully immersed?

❏ What does the line of demarcation look like?

❏ Are there any splash burns present?

❏ How symmetrical are the lines of immersion if stocking or glove patterns are present?

❏ Is toilet training, soiling, or wetting an issue?

❏ Have you recorded information concerning the child's age, height, degree of development and coordination; location of fixtures; temperature and depth of water; weight of burn object, etc.?

❏ Have you compared the burn injury with the area of sparing?

❏ Was the child in a state of flexion (tensing of the body parts in reaction to what was happening) indicating resistance? Examples of flexion on a child's body include:

☐ Folds in the stomach.

☐ Calf against back of thigh.

☐ Arms tightened and held firmly against body or folded against body.

☐ Thighs against abdomen.

☐ Head against shoulder.

☐ Legs crossed, held tightly together.

Reenactment of the Incident

Objectivity is without a doubt the most important quality you should possess as an investigator. Reenacting the incident as given to you by the witness is a good way to obtain objective information and to answer any questions you may have. Using yourself or another adult, but never the child, you can reenact the incident at the scene, at your home or office, and, ultimately, in court as demonstrative evidence. The following are examples of useful reenactment of the incident:

✳ When investigating wet contact injuries, use water with blue dye to re-create the incident and then photograph the results, which often clearly show that the child's burn injury pattern is not consistent with the pattern that would have resulted from the described incident.

✳ The fact that the time of exposure, temperature of the water, and degree of the burn are all related will test the accuracy of the caretaker's reenactment of the incident.

✳ If the suspect re-creates the incident using cooler water, thinking that if hot water is used it will look incriminating, you can point out that if the water had been at that temperature, the child would have to have been held still for a long time in order to receive the degree of injury sustained.

Another example is a burn that a witness claims happened because the child was playing with a disposable cigarette lighter. Cigarette lighters cause a specific injury pattern. Take an inkpad, re-create the top of the lighter on a piece of paper, and note the pattern. Next, using the inkpad, re-create the pattern on different parts of your body. You will see that it is difficult to make an impression without distorting the pattern and that the pattern is different on soft tissue as opposed to hard, bony parts.

Moreover, if the lighter has a safety switch, as most disposable lighters now do, could the injured child have released the safety switch, lit the lighter, kept the flame lit, and burned the area of the body that was injured without burning his or her own hand, especially the thumb closest to the flame?

Documentation

The following elements are important in diagramming and photographing the scene:

✳ When diagramming, be sure to include all items in the room where the incident occurred. Children often climb when they are exploring. You may think the sink is too high for access by the child, but a determined child may have climbed from a step stool, to the toilet seat, to a hamper, and then the sink.

* Accurate measurements of the items involved in the incident — tub, basin, stove height, height to object, etc. — are essential. Photographs of these items should document the size and shape of the item and should contain a measure scale.

* Always use color 35mm film for photographs. It will give you maximum clarity and detail and is best suited for making enlargements for court evidence. Instant cameras are acceptable but do not give the same clarity and produce photographs less suitable for enlargements.

All body parts should be photographed. Photographs should include a standard front, standard back, standard left, and standard right. The significantly burned areas should be particularly well photographed. Reliable testimony, however, should not be based solely on photographs or drawings. Testimony from the treating physician or medical personnel who conducted a hands-on evaluation of the child is critical and more effective.

Working With Other Agencies

Fire and rescue teams are usually the first responders to a 911 call for a burn victim. Their observations of the scene and their communication tapes verifying the response time provide valuable information.

Another important agency is the Department of Social Services. It is advisable to work closely with the child protection services team, for their cooperation can result in evidence and information law enforcement may not be aware of. In fact, joint training sessions of social services, medical, emergency response, and prosecutorial personnel can benefit everyone — victim and investigators.

Contributing Authors

Phylip J. Peltier
Criminal Investigator
Butte County District Attorney's Office
Special Victims Unit
25 County Center Drive
Oroville, CA 95965
530–538–5224

Gary Purdue, M.D.
Professor, Department of Surgery
The University of Texas
Southwestern Medical Center
5323 Harry Hines Boulevard
Dallas, TX 75390–9158
214–648–2041

Captain Jack R. Shepherd
Commander, Executive Division
Office of the Director
Michigan State Police
714 South Harrison Road
East Lansing, MI 48823
517–336–6552

Supplemental Reading

Besharov DJ. *Combating Child Abuse: Guidelines for Cooperation Between Law Enforcement and Child Protective Agencies.* Washington, DC: AEI Press, 1990.

Butler KD, Chadwick DL. Child abuse. In Warner CG (ed): *Emergency Care: Assessment and Intervention.* 2d ed. St. Louis, MO: Mosby, 1978.

Deitch EA, Staats M. Child abuse through burning. *Journal of Burn Care and Rehabilitation* 3:89–94, 1982.

DePanfilis D, Salus MK. *A Coordinated Response to Child Abuse and Neglect: A Basic Manual* (The User Manual Series). Washington, DC: U.S. Department of Health and Human Services, Administration on Children, Youth and Families, National Center on Child Abuse and Neglect, 1992.

Fowler J. Child maltreatment by burning. *Burns* 5:83–85, 1978.

Gary FP, Hunt JL, Prescott PR. Child abuse by burning— An index of suspicion. *Journal of Trauma* 28(2):221–224, 1988.

Gil DG. *Violence Against Children: Physical Child Abuse in the United States.* Cambridge, MA: Harvard University Press, 1970.

Helfer RE, Kempe RS (eds). *The Battered Child*. 4th ed. Chicago, IL: University of Chicago Press, 1987.

Hight DW, Bakalar HR, Lloyd JR. Inflicted burns in children: Recognition and treatment. *Journal of the American Medical Association* 242:517–520, 1979.

Lenoski EF, Hunter KA. Specific patterns of inflicted burn injuries. *Journal of Trauma* 17:842–846, 1977.

MacMillan BG, Freiberg DL. Special problems of the pediatric burn patient. In Hummel RP (ed): *Clinical Burn Therapy*. Boston (MA), Bristol, and London: John Wright/ PSG Inc., 1982.

Moritz AR, Henriques FC. Studies of thermal injury: II. The relative importance of time and surface temperature in the causation of cutaneous burns. *American Journal of Pathology* 23:695–720, 1947.

Pence D, Wilson C. *The Role of Law Enforcement in the Response to Child Abuse and Neglect* (The User Manual Series). Washington, DC: U.S. Department of Health and Human Services, Administration on Children, Youth and Families, National Center on Child Abuse and Neglect, 1992.

Purdue GF, Hunt JL. Child abuse by burning. In Ludwig S, Kornberg A (eds): *Child Abuse: A Medical Reference*. New York, NY: Churchill Livingstone, 1992, pp. 105–116.

Schanberger JE. Inflicted burns in children. *Topics in Emergency Medicine* 3:85–92, 1981.

Shepherd JR, Dworin B, Farley RH, Russ BJ, Tressler PW, National Center for Missing and Exploited Children. *Child Abuse and Exploitation: Investigative Techniques*. 2d ed. Washington, DC: Office of Juvenile Justice and Delinquency Prevention, 1995.

Stone NH, Rinaldo L, Humphrey CR, et al. Child abuse by burning. *Surgical Clinics of North America* 50:1419–1424, 1974.

Whitcomb D. *When the Victim Is a Child*. 2d ed. Washington, DC: U.S. Department of Justice, Office of Justice Programs, National Institute of Justice, 1992.

Organizations

American Burn Association
800–548–2876

Fox Valley Technical College
Criminal Justice Department
Law Enforcement Training Programs
P.O. Box 2277
1825 North Bluemound Drive
Appleton, WI 54914–2277
800–648–4966
920–735–4757 (fax)
http://www.foxvalley.tec.wi.us/ojjdp

Participants are trained in child abuse and exploitation investigative techniques, covering the following areas: recognition of signs of abuse, collection and preservation of evidence, preparation of cases for prosecution, techniques for interviewing victims and offenders, and liability issues.

Fox Valley also offers an intensive special training for local child investigative teams. Teams must include representatives from law enforcement, prosecution, social services, and (optionally) the medical field. Participants take part in hands-on team activity involving:

* Development of interagency processes and protocols for enhanced enforcement, prevention, and intervention in child abuse cases.

* Case preparation and prosecution.

* Development of the team's own interagency implementation plan for improved investigation of child abuse.

National Burn Victim Foundation
246A Madisonville Road
Basking Ridge, NJ 07920
800–803–5879
908–953–9091
908–953–9099 (fax)

The Phoenix Society for Burn Survivors, Inc.
2153 Wealthy Street SE., Suite 215
East Grand Rapids, MI 49506
616–458–2773
Burn survivor toll-free line: 800–888–BURN
Burn camps in the United States and abroad: 800–888–BURN
http://www.phoenix-society.org

Shriners Hospital Referral Line
2900 Rocky Point Drive
Tampa, FL 33607
800–237–5055

Shriners Burn Institutes

Boston Unit
51 Blossom Street
Boston, MA 02114
617–722–3000

Cincinnati Unit
3229 Burnet Avenue
Cincinnati, OH 45229
513–872–6000

Galveston Unit
815 Market Street
Galveston, TX 77550
409–770–6600

Sacramento Unit
2425 Stockton Boulevard
Sacramento, CA 95817
916–453–2000

Trauma Burn Center
University of Michigan Medical Center
1500 East Medical Center Drive
Ann Arbor, MI 48109–0033
734–936–9666

In addition, many communities have their own burn centers, which can be identified through local hospitals.

---

*R*ecord the name, location, and number of your nearest burn trauma unit here.

_____

_____

_____

(_____) _____

Instructions for Evidence Worksheet
for Immersion Burns

Section A

The location should include the address and room in which the burn occurred.

Section B

Two investigators are required to gather the information on the worksheet. You will need an immersion thermometer, a 35mm camera, a measuring device, and a watch with a second hand.

Photograph the scene with a 35mm camera. Use a ruler, yardstick, or tape measure in all photographs.

Sketch the scene including all objects in the area. Be sure to include the distance from the basin or tub in relation to nearby objects and the dimensions of furniture, fixtures, etc.

Section C

One investigator holds the thermometer so that the water from the faucet is hitting at the immersion line on the thermometer. That person notes the starting temperature, which is recorded by the other investigator, who is also holding the watch. The first investigator calls out the time and the second investigator calls out the temperature in response, recording it at 5-second intervals (or when the temperature remains constant for 15 seconds). **Note:** The person holding the thermometer should not be wearing glasses since the steam will fog them up.

When recording the hot and cold water temperature together, turn the faucets on full and record when the temperature remains constant for 15 seconds.

Section D

After the tub or basin is filled, you can hold a low-key interview with the caretaker and/or witnesses while checking the temperature at 5-minute intervals.

Section E

Have the suspect show you how he or she ran the water when the burn occurred. If the suspect wants to run the water deeper than 5 inches, allow this and note it on the worksheet.

EVIDENCE WORKSHEET FOR IMMERSION BURNS

A	Case No.
	Present Date:
	Suspect's Name:
	Victim's Name:
	Incident Location (within dwelling):
	Address:
	City/State/Zip:

B

Bathtub Measurements (measurements should be made in inches)

Width:	Inside Depth:
Top Length:	Bottom Length:

Construction (porcelain, fiberglass, plastic, etc.)

C

Running Water Temperatures (in Fahrenheit)

HOT		COLD	
Seconds	**Degrees**	**Seconds**	**Degrees**
0	_____	_____	_____
5	_____	Running Water Temperature	
10	_____	(Full Hot and Cold)	
20	_____	Seconds _____ Peak Temp. _____	
_____	_____		

D

Full Tub; Standing Hot Water, 5 Inches Deep
(temperature measured in middle of tub at water mid-depth)

FILL TIME			
Inches	**Minutes/Seconds**	**Minutes**	**Degrees**
1	_____	0	_____
2	_____	5	_____
3	_____	10	_____
4	_____	15	_____
5	_____	20	_____
		25	_____
		30	_____

E

_____ ran a tub of water on my request.
Results: Depth 5 inches. One minute after water off: Temperature
_____ degrees Fahrenheit.

Investigator #1 _____ ID# _____ Division _____
Investigator #2 _____ ID# _____ Division _____

Source: Phylip J. Peltier, Criminal Investigator, Oroville, California

Other Titles in This Series

Currently there are 12 other Portable Guides to Investigating Child Abuse. Additional guides in this series may be developed at a later date. To obtain a copy of any of the guides listed below (in order of publication), contact the Office of Juvenile Justice and Delinquency Prevention's Juvenile Justice Clearinghouse by telephone at 800–638–8736 or e-mail at puborder@ncjrs.org.

Recognizing When a Child's Injury or Illness Is Caused by Abuse, NCJ 160938

Sexually Transmitted Diseases and Child Sexual Abuse, NCJ 160940

Photodocumentation in the Investigation of Child Abuse, NCJ 160939

Diagnostic Imaging of Child Abuse, NCJ 161235

Battered Child Syndrome: Investigating Physical Abuse and Homicide, NCJ 161406

Interviewing Child Witnesses and Victims of Sexual Abuse, NCJ 161623

Child Neglect and Munchausen Syndrome by Proxy, NCJ 161841

Criminal Investigation of Child Sexual Abuse, NCJ 162426

Law Enforcement Response to Child Abuse, NCJ 162425

Understanding and Investigating Child Sexual Exploitation, NCJ 162427

Forming a Multidisciplinary Team To Investigate Child Abuse, NCJ 170020

Use of Computers in the Sexual Exploitation of Children, NCJ 170021

Additional Resources

American Bar Association
(ABA)
Center on Children and
the Law
Washington, DC
202–662–1720
202–662–1755 (fax)

American Humane Association
Englewood, Colorado
800–227–4645
303–792–9900
303–792–5333 (fax)

American Medical Association
(AMA)
Department of Mental Health
Chicago, Illinois
312–464–5000
(AMA main number)
312–464–4184 (fax)

American Professional Society
on the Abuse of Children
(APSAC)
Oklahoma City, Oklahoma
405–271–8202
405–271–2931 (fax)

Federal Bureau of Investigation
(FBI)
National Center for the
Analysis of Violent Crime
Quantico, Virginia
703–632–4333

Fox Valley Technical College
Criminal Justice Department
Appleton, Wisconsin
800–648–4966
920–735–4757 (fax)

Juvenile Justice Clearinghouse
(JJC)
Rockville, Maryland
800–638–8736
301–519–5600 (fax)

Kempe Children's Center
Denver, Colorado
303–864–5252
303–864–5302 (fax)

National Association of Medical
Examiners
St. Louis, Missouri
314–577–8298
314–268–5124 (fax)

National Center for Missing
and Exploited Children
(NCMEC)
Alexandria, Virginia
703–274–3900
703–274–2220 (fax)

National Center for the
Prosecution of Child Abuse
Alexandria, Virginia
703–549–4253
703–549–6259 (fax)

National Children's Alliance
Washington, DC
800–239–9950
202–639–0597
202–639–0511 (fax)

National Clearinghouse on
Child Abuse and Neglect
Information
Washington, DC
800–FYI–3366
703–385–7565
703–385–3206 (fax)

National SIDS Resource
Center
Vienna, Virginia
703–821–8955, ext. 249
703–821–2098 (fax)

Prevent Child Abuse America
Chicago, Illinois
800–835–2671
312–663–3520
312–939–8962 (fax)

www.ingramcontent.com/pod-product-compliance
Lightning Source LLC
Chambersburg PA
CBHW071604170526
45166CB00004B/1794